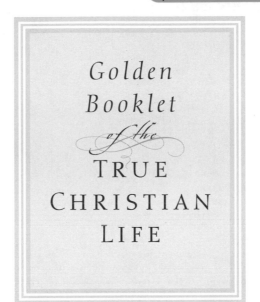

Golden Booklet *of the* TRUE CHRISTIAN LIFE

JOHN CALVIN

*A Modern Translation
from the French and the Latin
by*
Henry J. Van Andel

BakerBooks
a division of Baker Publishing Group
Grand Rapids, Michigan

© 1952 by Baker Book House Company

Published by Baker Books
a division of Baker Publishing Group
P.O. Box 6287, Grand Rapids, MI 49516-6287
www.bakerbooks.com

Paperback edition published 2004
ISBN 978-0-8010-6528-6

Printed in the United States of America

The Library of Congress has cataloged the hardcover edition as follows:
Calvin, Jean, 1509–1564
    [De vita hominis Christiani. English]
    Golden booklet of the true Christian life / John Calvin ; a modern translation from the French and the Latin by Henry J. Van Andel.
        p.   cm.
    Originally published: 1952.
    ISBN 0-8010-1249-X
    1. Christian Life. I. Van Andel, Henry J. II. Title.
BV4501.3 .C35513
248.4p842—dc21   2002009996

Scripture is taken from the King James Version of the Bible.

15   16   17   12   11   10   9   8

Contents

Contents

CHAPTER III

Patience
in Crossbearing

Preface

The *Golden Booklet of the True Christian Walk* was first published in 1550 in Latin and in French under the title *De Vita Hominis Christiani*, that is, *On the Life of the Christian Man* (the present heading of Chapter Six, Book III, of the *Institutes*), and later also in English (1594) and in German (1857) under a similar name. In Dutch it appeared in 1858 with the first mentioned title. Originally the *Golden Booklet* was not a separate volume, but part of the *Institutes*. It was missing in the short first edition, but in the second, third, and fourth editions it occurred as the last or twenty-first chapter, called *De Vita Christiana* ("On the Christian Life"). In the fifth and sixth editions Calvin rearranged the material of the *Institutes* under four headings: the Father, the Son, the Holy Spirit, and the Church. He placed the thoroughly revised material "On the Christian Life" halfway through Book III and divided it into five parts, chapters six to ten inclusive. The *Institutes* were often reprinted both in Latin and in other languages, and some portions were published separately, but the *Golden Booklet* alone had the honor of being reprinted four times in Dutch, the last reprint being in 1938. The present American edition is a translation of Calvin's thoroughly revised copy and is based on the French and Latin texts of the *Golden Booklet* (*Inst.* III, Chs. 6 to 10, sixth edition).

This *Booklet* was purposely written in a simpler style than the other parts of the *Institutes*. On account of its spiritual and realistic nature it made an indelible impression on the Dutch nation which had brought forth such famous writers as John van Ruysbroec and Thomas à Kempis during the Christian Renaissance (1350–1500). But it must also have made a tremendous appeal to the Pilgrims and the Puritans and to all groups which felt the need of a balanced application of Christianity. Calvin directs himself to mind, heart, and hand, for he is the first one to elaborate on the three offices of Christ. He is intellectual, mystical, and practical. His basic principles satisfied many scholars, religious leaders, and statesmen. But there is, on the other hand, no other devotional book in the world like the *Golden Booklet* which is so profound and yet so universal. As to style, spirit, and graphic language it can vie with the great classics, like Augustine's *Confessions,* Thomas à Kempis's *Imitation of Christ,* and Bunyan's *Pilgrim's Progress.* Only it is shorter, saner, sounder, more vigorous and to the point. It should, therefore, be welcomed by all people of a genuine religious nature, but especially by those who want to carry out the values of religion in everyday life.

Although this new translation is modern, the classical text has been adhered to as closely as possible. The editor has, however, taken the liberty of giving some chapters a title more in agreement with their content; he has also given every section a heading, divided the sections into smaller units, and added a few scriptural references in brackets.

A brief biographical note may be of interest here. John Calvin was born in 1509 in northern France, in the city of Noyon, and died in Geneva, Switzerland, in 1564. He was educated in the classics and philosophy, in law and theology in the colleges and universities of his native land. When persecution came he fled to Basel, in Switzerland, where he wrote the first edition of his *Institutes* when he was only twenty-six years of age. Then he went to visit the Duchess of Ferrara, the sister of the French king, in northern Italy because she gave shelter to a number of Reformed refugees. On his way back from Italy to Basel he was pressed into service by his friend Farel to help reform Geneva. Here Calvin founded not a new state but a new church, the Reformed or Presbyterian church, and a new school system with a famous university. In the Academy or graduate department of this new university he became a professor of theology.

In his short life Calvin wrote fifty-eight volumes, some in Latin and some in French. His works are not only of a theological nature, but many contain ethical and philosophical principles that laid the foundation for a new system of thought. His *Institutes* was a textbook for dogmatics, ethics, and philosophy for two hundred years. He found thousands of ardent followers in the western countries of Europe, but also in Hungary, the Ukraine, and Poland. His greatest influence was felt in Switzerland, the Rhine valley, the Netherlands, England and Scotland, and last, but not least, in North America. Calvin's commentaries on the Bible have become so famous that they have been newly reprinted in America. His *Institutes* has again become a textbook in many colleges and seminaries. His ideas are being studied by those who do not fully agree with his basic concepts. John Calvin was a man of a gentle nature and of colossal stature. He is now becoming the leading figure of Orthodox Protestantism in Europe and America.

Henry J. Van Andel
Calvin College, Grand Rapids, Michigan, 1952

Prayer of Calvin

Almighty God and Father, grant unto us, because we have to go through much strife on this earth, the strength of thy Holy Spirit, in order that we may courageously go through the fire, and through the water, and that we may put ourselves so under thy rule that we may go to meet death in full confidence of thy assistance and without fear.

Grant us also that we may bear all hatred and enmity of mankind, until we have gained the last victory, and that we may at last come to that blessed rest which thy only begotten Son has acquired for us through his blood. Amen.

Live in submission w/ His sovereignty

* The law is beautiful
  - obedience
  - loved / excepted & believing

Luther
Liberty from
the law

Holiness is central

↓

... living out the Gift

attain
Submission
living in the future

CHAPTER I

Humble Obedience, the True Imitation of Christ

I. Scripture is the rule of life.

1. The goal of the new life is that God's children exhibit melody and harmony in their conduct. What melody? The song of God's justice. What harmony? The harmony between God's righteousness and our obedience.

Only if we walk in the beauty of God's law do we become sure of our adoption as children of the Father.

The law of God contains in itself the dynamic of the new life by which his image is fully restored in us; but by nature we are sluggish, and, therefore, we need to be stimulated, aided in our efforts by a guiding principle.

A sincere repentance from the heart does not guarantee that we shall not wander from the straight path and sometimes become bewildered.

Let us then search Scripture to find the root principle for the reformation of our life.

2. Scripture contains a great number of exhortations, and to discuss them all would fill a large volume.

The church fathers have written big works on the virtues without prating; even a scholarly treatise cannot exhaust the profundity of one virtue.

For true devotion, however, it is not necessary to read the excellent works of the church fathers, but only to understand the one basic rule of the Bible.[1]

3. No one should draw the conclusion that the brevity of one treatise on Christian conduct makes the elaborate discussion of others superfluous, or that philosophy has no value.

Philosophers, however, are accustomed to speak of general principles and specific rules, but Scripture has an order all its own.

Philosophers are ambitious, and, therefore, aim at exquisite clarity and dexterous ingenuity; but Scripture has a beautiful conciseness, and a certainty which excels all philosophers.

Philosophers often make a show of affectation, but the Holy Spirit has a different method [direct and plainspoken] which ought not to be neglected.[2]

II. Holiness is the key principle.

1. The plan of Scripture for a Christian walk is twofold: first, that we be instructed in the law to love righteousness, because by nature we are not inclined to do so; second, that we be shown a simple rule that we may not waver in our race.

Of the many excellent recommendations, is there any better than the key principle: Be thou holy, for I am holy?

When we were dispersed like scattered sheep, and lost in the labyrinth of the world, Christ gathered us together again, that he might bring us back to himself.

2. When we hear any mention of our mystical union with Christ, we should remember that holiness is the channel to it.

Justification by faith

Holiness is not a merit by which we can attain communion with God, but a gift of Christ, which enables us to cling to him, and to follow him.

It is God's own glory that he cannot have anything to do

Murry - Union w/ Christ (marriage)
Holiness is the portal

with iniquity and uncleanness; therefore, we must keep this in mind if we desire to pay attention to his invitation.

For why were we delivered from the quagmire of iniquity and pollution of this world, if we want to wallow in it as long as we live?

God's holiness admonishes us that we must inhabit the holy city of Jerusalem if we wish to belong to the people of God.

Jerusalem is hallowed ground, therefore it cannot be profaned by impure inhabitants.

The Psalmist says, "This one shall abide in the tabernacle of the Lord who walks uprightly and works righteousness."

The sanctuary of the Holy One must be kept immaculate (Lev. 19:2; 1 Pet. 1:16; Isa. 35:10; Ps. 15:1–2; 24:3–4).

III. Holiness means full obedience to Christ.

1. Scripture does not only show the principle of holiness, but also that Christ is the way to it.

Because the Father has reconciled us to himself in Christ, therefore he commands us to be conformed to Christ as to our pattern.

Let those who think that philosophers have the only just and orderly system of morality show us a more excellent plan than to obey and follow Christ.

The sublimest virtue according to philosophers is to live

the life of nature, but Scripture points us to the perfect Christ as our example.

We should exhibit the character of Christ in our lives, for what can be more effective than this one stirring consideration? Indeed, what can be required besides?

2. The Lord has adopted us to be his children on this condition that we reveal an imitation of Christ who is the mediator of our adoption.

Unless we ardently and prayerfully devote ourselves to Christ's righteousness we do not only faithlessly revolt from our Creator, but we also abjure him as our Savior.

3. Scripture accompanies its exhortations with the promise of God's countless blessings and of the all-embracing salvation he grants us.

Therefore, since God has revealed himself as a Father, we would be guilty of the basest ingratitude if we did not behave as his children.

Since Christ has purified us through the baptism in his blood, we should not become defiled by fresh pollution.

Since Christ has united us to his body as his members, we should be anxious not to disgrace him by any blemish.

Since Christ, our Head, has ascended to heaven, we should leave our carnal desires behind and lift our hearts upward to him.

Since the Holy Spirit has dedicated us as temples of God,

we should exert ourselves not to profane his sanctuary, but to display his glory.

Since both our soul and body are destined to inherit an incorruptible and never-fading crown, we should keep them pure and undefiled till the day of our Lord.

Such are the best foundations for a proper code of conduct. Philosophers never rise above the natural dignity of man. (But Scripture points us to our only sinless Savior, Jesus Christ. Rom. 6:4ff; 8:29)

IV. External Christianity is not enough.

1. Let us ask those who possess nothing but church membership, and yet want to be called Christians, how they can glory in the sacred name of Christ?

For no one has any communion with Christ but he who has received the true knowledge of him from the word of the gospel.

The apostle denies that anyone actually knows Christ who has not learned to put off the old man, corrupt with deceitful lusts, and to put on Christ.

External knowledge of Christ is found to be only a false and dangerous make-believe, however eloquently and freely lip servants may talk about the gospel.

2. The gospel is not a doctrine of the tongue, but of life.

HEART CHANGE

It cannot be grasped by reason and memory only, but it is fully understood when it possesses the whole soul and penetrates to the inner recesses of the heart.

Let nominal Christians cease from insulting God by boasting themselves to be what they are not, and let them show themselves disciples not unworthy of Christ, their Master.

We must assign first place to the knowledge of our religion, for that is the beginning of our salvation.

But our religion will be unprofitable if it does not change our heart, pervade our manners, and transform us into new creatures.

3. The philosophers rightly condemn and banish with disgrace from their company those who profess to know the art of life, but who are in reality vain babblers.

With much better reason Christians ought to detest those who have the gospel on their lips but not in their hearts.

The exhortations of the philosophers are cold and lifeless if compared with the convictions, affections, and boundless energy of the real believers (Eph. 4:22ff).

V. Spiritual progress is necessary.

1. We should not insist on absolute perfection of the gospel in our fellow Christians, however much we may strive for it ourselves.

It would be unfair to demand evangelical perfection before we acknowledge anyone as a Christian.

There would be no church if we set a standard of absolute perfection, for the best of us are still far from the ideal, and we would have to reject many who have made only small progress.

2. Perfection must be the final mark at which we aim, and the goal for which we strive.

It is not lawful for you to make a compromise with God: to try to fulfill part of your duties and to omit others at your own pleasure.

The Lord first of all wants sincerity in his service, simplicity of heart without guile and falsehood.

A double mind is in conflict with the spiritual life, for this implies an unfeigned devotion to God in the search for holiness and righteousness.

No one in this earthly prison of the body has sufficient strength of his own to press forward with a due degree of watchfulness, and the great majority [of Christians] are kept down with such great weakness that they stagger and halt and even creep on the ground, and so make very slight advances.

3. But let everyone proceed according to his given ability and continue the journey he has begun.

There is no man so unhappy that he will not make some progress, however small.

Let us not cease to do the utmost, that we may incessantly go forward in the way of the Lord; and let us not despair because of the smallness of our accomplishment.

Though we fall short, our labor is not lost if this day surpasses the preceding one.

4. The one condition for spiritual progress is that we remain sincere and humble.

Let us keep our end in view, let us press forward to our goal. Let us not indulge in pride, nor give in to our sinful passions.

Let us steadily exert ourselves to reach a higher degree of holiness till we shall finally arrive at a perfection of goodness which we seek and pursue as long as we live, but which we shall attain then only, when, freed from all earthly infirmity, we shall be admitted by God into his full communion.

CHAPTER II

Self-Denial

I. We are not our own, we are the Lord's.

1. The divine law contains a most fitting and well ordered plan for the regulation of our life; yet it has pleased the heavenly Teacher to direct men by a very excellent key principle.

It is the duty of believers to "present their bodies a living sacrifice, holy, acceptable unto God"; this is the only true worship.

The principle of holiness leads to the exhortation, "Be not conformed to this world; but be ye transformed by the renewing of your mind, that ye may prove what is the will of God."

It is a very important consideration that we are consecrated and dedicated to God; it means that we may think, speak, meditate, or do anything only with a view to his glory.

For that which is sacred cannot, without great injustice to God, be applied to unholy usage.

Matt 16:24

2. If we are not our own, but the Lord's, it is plain what error we must flee, and to what purpose all our deeds must be directed.

We are not our own, therefore neither our reason nor our will should guide us in our thoughts and actions.

We are not our own, therefore we should not seek what is expedient to the flesh.

We are not our own, therefore let us forget ourselves and our own interests as far as possible.

But we are God's own; to him, therefore, let us live and die.

We are God's own; therefore let his wisdom and will dominate all our actions.

We are God's own; therefore let every part of our existence be directed toward him as our only legitimate goal.

3. Oh, how greatly has the man advanced who has learned not to be his own, not to be governed by his own reason, but to surrender his mind to God!

The most effective poison to lead men to ruin is to boast in themselves, in their own wisdom and willpower; the only escape to safety is simply to follow the guidance of the Lord.

Our first step should be to take leave of ourselves and to apply all our powers to the service of the Lord.

4. The service of the Lord does not only include implicit obedience, but also a willingness to put aside our sinful desires, and to surrender completely to the leadership of the Holy Spirit.

The transformation of our lives by the Holy Spirit, which Paul calls a renewal of the mind, is the real beginning of life, but foreign to pagan philosophers.

Pagan philosophers set up reason as the sole guide of life, of wisdom and conduct; but Christian philosophy demands of us that we surrender our reason to the Holy Spirit; and this means that we no longer live for ourselves, but that Christ lives and reigns within us (Rom. 12:1; Eph. 4:23; Gal. 2:20).

Fruits of submission

SELF DENIAL

II. Seeking God's glory means self-denial.

1. Let us therefore not seek our own but that which pleases the Lord, and is helpful to the promotion of his glory.

There is a great advantage in almost forgetting ourselves and in surely neglecting all selfish aspects; for then only can we try faithfully to devote our attention to God and his commandments.

For when Scripture tells us to discard all personal and selfish considerations, it does not only exclude from our minds the desire for wealth, the lust of power, and the favor of men, but it also banishes false ambitions and hunger for human glory with other more secret evils.

Indeed, a Christian ought to be disposed and prepared to keep in mind that he has to reckon with God every moment of his life.

2. A Christian will measure all his deeds by God's law, and his secret thoughts he will subject to God's will.

If a man has learned to regard God in every enterprise, he will be delivered from all vain desires.

The denial of ourselves which Christ has so diligently commanded his disciples from the beginning will at last dominate all the desires of our heart.

The denial of ourselves will leave no room for pride, haughtiness, or vainglory, nor for avarice, licentiousness, love of luxury, wantonness, or any sin born from self-love.

Without the principle of self-denial man is either led to indulgence in the grossest vices without the least shame; or, if there is any appearance of virtue in him, it is spoiled by an evil passion for glory.

Show me a single man who does not believe in the Lord's law of self-denial, and who yet willingly practices virtue among men.

3. All who have not been influenced by the principle of self-denial, have followed virtue merely from the love of praise.

Even those of the philosophers who have contended that

virtue is desirable for its own sake, have been puffed up with so much arrogance, that it is evident they desire virtue for no other reason than to give them a chance to exercise pride.

God is so far from being pleased either with those who are ambitious of popular praise, or with hearts full of pride and presumption, that he plainly tells "they have their reward" in this world, and that (repentant) harlots and publicans are nearer to the kingdom of heaven than such persons.

4. There is no end and no limit to the obstacles of the man who wants to pursue what is right and at the same time shrinks back from self-denial.

It is an ancient and true observation that there is a world of vices hidden in the soul of man, but Christian self-denial is the remedy of them all.

There is deliverance in store only for the man who gives up his selfishness, and whose sole aim is to please the Lord and to do what is right in his sight.

III. Self-denial means: sobriety, righteousness, and godliness.

1. The apostle Paul gives a brief summary of a well regulated life when he says to Titus: "The grace of God that brings salvation has appeared to all men, teaching us, that denying ungodliness and worldly lusts, we should live soberly, righ-

teously, and godly in this present world; looking for that blessed hope, and the glorious appearing of the great God and our Savior Jesus Christ who gave himself for us, that he might redeem us from all iniquity and purify unto himself a peculiar people, zealous of good works."

Paul declares that the grace of God is necessary to stimulate us, but that for true worship two main obstacles must be removed: first, ungodliness to which we are by nature strongly inclined, and then, worldly lusts which try to overwhelm us.

Ungodliness does not only mean superstitions, but everything that hinders the sincere fear of God. And worldly lusts mean carnal affections.

Paul urges us to forsake our former desires which are in conflict with the two tables of the law, and to renounce all the dictates of our own reason and will.

2. Paul reduces all the actions of the new life to three classes: sobriety, righteousness, and godliness.

Sobriety undoubtedly means chastity and temperance, as well as the pure and frugal use of temporal blessings and patience under poverty.

Righteousness includes all the duties of justice, that every man may receive his just dues.

Godliness separates us from the pollutions of the world, and by true holiness unites us to God.

When the virtues of sobriety, righteousness, and godliness are firmly linked together, they will produce absolute perfection.

3. Nothing is more difficult than to forsake all carnal thoughts, to subdue and renounce our false appetites, and to devote ourselves to God and our brethren, and to live the life of angels in a world of corruption.

To deliver our minds from every snare Paul calls our attention to the hope of a blessed immortality, and encourages us that our hope is not in vain.

As Christ once appeared as a Redeemer, so he will at his second coming show us the benefits of the salvation which he obtained.

Christ dispels the charms that blind us and prevent us from longing with the right zeal for the glory of heaven.

Christ also teaches us that we must live as strangers and pilgrims in this world, that we may not lose our heavenly inheritance (Titus 2:11–14).

IV. True humility means respect for others.

1. Self-denial refers partly to men, but indeed, principally to God.

When Scripture commands us to conduct ourselves in such a manner toward men, as "in honor to prefer others to ourselves," and faithfully to devote our whole attention to the promotion of their advantage, it gives such commands as our heart can by no means receive without being first cured of our sinful nature.

We are all so blinded and upset by self-love that everyone imagines he has a just right to exalt himself and to undervalue all others in comparison to self.

If God has bestowed on us any excellent gift, we imagine it to be our own achievement; and we swell and even burst with pride.

2. The vices of which we are full we carefully hide from others, and we flatter ourselves with the notion that they are small and trivial; we sometimes even embrace them as virtues.

If the same talents which we admire in ourselves appear in others, or even our betters, we depreciate and diminish them with the utmost malignity, in order that we may not have to acknowledge the superiority of others.

If others have any vices, we are not content to criticize them sharply and severely, but we exaggerate them hatefully.

Hatred grows into insolence when we desire to excel the rest of mankind and imagine we do not belong to the common lot; we even severely and haughtily despise others as our inferiors.

3. The poor yield to the rich, the common people to the upper ten, the servants to their masters, the ignorant to the scholars; but there is nobody who does not imagine that he is really better than the others.

Everyone flatters himself and carries a kingdom in his breast.

pride

Everyone is self-complacent and passes censure on the ideas and conduct of others, and if there is a quarrel there is an eruption of poison.

Many discover some gentleness in others as long as they find everything pleasant and amiable; but how many keep their good humor if they are disturbed and irritated?

4. To live happily the evils of false ambition and self-love must be plucked from our hearts by the roots.

If we listen to the instruction of Scripture, we must remember that our talents are not of our own making, but free gifts of God.

If we are proud of our talents, we betray our lack of gratitude to God.

"Who makes you to differ?" says Paul. "Now, if you received all gifts, why do you glory as if you had not received them?"

We must watch and acknowledge our faults, and be truly humble. For then we shall not be puffed up, but have great reason to feel dejected.

5. On the other hand, whatever gifts of God we notice in others, let us value and esteem both the gifts and their possessors, for it would betray great wickedness in us to rob them of their God-given honor.

The faults of others we are taught to overlook, not to encourage them by flattery.

We should never insult others on account of their faults, for it is our duty to show charity and respect to everyone.

If we pay attention to the honor and reputation of others, whoever they may be, we shall conduct ourselves not only with moderation and good humor, but with politeness and friendship.

For we shall never arrive at true meekness by any other way than by humiliating ourselves and by honoring others from the depth of our hearts (Rom. 12:10; Phil. 2:4; 1 Cor. 4:7). *good verses for being a manager*

V. We should seek the good of other believers.

1. How extremely difficult it is for you dutifully to seek the advantage of your neighbor, unless you quit all selfish considerations and almost forget yourself.

How can you perform the duties which Paul teaches to be works of love, unless you renounce yourself and devote yourself wholly to others? "Love suffers long and is kind; love envies not; love vaunts not itself; love is not puffed up; love does not behave itself unseemly; love seeks not her own; love is not easily provoked"; and so on.

2. If this be all that is demanded, that we do not seek our own, yet we must not exert little pressure in our own nature, which is so strongly inclined to love self exclusively and does not easily permit us to neglect self and our own affairs.

Let us rather seek the profit of others, and even voluntarily give up our rights for the sake of others.

Scripture urges and warns us that whatever favors we may have obtained from the Lord, we have received them as a trust on condition that they should be applied to the common benefit of the church.

The legitimate use of all the Lord's favors is liberally and kindly to share them with others.

You cannot imagine a more certain rule or a more powerful suggestion than this, that all the blessings we enjoy are divine deposits which we have received on this condition that we distribute them to others.

3. According to Scripture our personal talents may be even compared to the powers of the members of the human body.

No member of the body has its power for itself, nor applies it to its own private use, but only for the profit of the others; and equally, no member of the church receives any advantage from his own activity, but through his cooperation with the whole body of believers.

Whatever ability a faithful Christian may possess, he ought to possess it for his fellow believers, and he ought to make his own interest subservient to the well-being of the church in all sincerity.

Let this be our rule for goodwill and helpfulness, that whenever we are able to assist others we should behave as stewards who must someday give an account of ourselves, and let us remember that the distribution of profits must be determined by the law of love.

For we must not first of all try to promote the good of others by seeking our own, but we must prefer the profit of others.

4. The law of love does not only pertain to the sizable profits, but from ancient days God has commanded us to remember it in the small kindnesses of life.

God commanded his people Israel to offer him the first-fruits of the corn, as a solemn token that it was unlawful for them to enjoy any blessings not previously dedicated to him.

If the gifts of God are not part of our sanctified life unless we dedicate them with our own hands to their Author, we must be guilty of sinful abuse if we leave such a dedication out.

5. But in vain we would attempt to enrich the Lord by a distribution of our talents and gifts.

Since our goodness cannot reach the Lord, as the Psalmist says, we must exercise it toward "the saints who are on the earth."

Alms are compared in the Scriptures to sacred offerings to show us that the exercises of charity under the gospel have taken the place of the sacrifices under the law of the Old Testament (1 Cor. 13:4–8; Ps. 16:2–3).

VI. We should seek the good of everyone, friend and foe.

1. That we may not become weary of doing well, for which the danger is near, the apostle has added that "love suffers long, and is not easily provoked."

The Lord commands us to do good unto all men without exception, though the majority are very undeserving when judged according to their own merits.

But Scripture here helps us out with an excellent argument when it teaches us that we must not think of man's real value, but only of his creation in the image of God to which we owe all possible honor and love.

The image of God, moreover, is most carefully to be regarded in those who are of the household of faith, because it has been renewed and restored in them by the Spirit of Christ.

2. If anyone, therefore, appears before you who is in need of your kind services, you have no reason to refuse him your help.

Suppose he is a stranger; yet the Lord has pressed his own stamp on him and made him as one of your family, and he forbids you to despise your own flesh and blood.

Suppose he is despicable and worthless; yet the Lord has deigned him worthy to be adorned with his own image.

Suppose that you have no obligation toward him for services; yet the Lord has made him as it were his substitute, so that you have obligation for numerous and unforgettable benefits.

Suppose that he is unworthy of your least exertion; but the image of God which recommends him to you deserves that you surrender yourself and all your possessions to him.

If he has deserved no kindness, but just the opposite, because he has maddened you with his injuries and insults, even this is no reason why you should not surround him with your affection and show him all sorts of favors.

You may say that he has deserved a very different treatment, but what does the Lord command but to forgive all men their offenses and to charge them against himself?

3. This is the only way to attain that which is not only difficult, but utterly repugnant to man's nature: to love those who hate us, to requite injuries with kindness, and to return blessings for curses.

We should forever keep in mind that we must not brood on the wickedness of man, but realize that he is God's image bearer.

If we cover and obliterate man's faults and consider the beauty and dignity of God's image in him, then we shall be induced to love and embrace him (Heb. 12:16; Gal. 6:10; Isa. 58:7; Matt. 5:44; Luke 17:3–4).

VII. Civil goodness is not enough.

1. We will not practice real self-denial unless we fulfill all the duties of love.

These are not fulfilled by him who merely in an external way performs his services without omitting even one, but by him who acts from a sincere principle of love.

For it may happen that a man discharges his duties to the best of his abilities, but if his heart is not in them, he falls far from the mark.

There are people who are known to be very liberal, yet they never give without scolding or pride or even insolence.

We are sunk to such a depth of calamity in this awful age that scarcely any alms are given, at least by the majority of men, without haughtiness and contempt.

The corruption of our times is so enormous that it would not have been tolerated by the pagans.

2. Christians certainly ought to display more than a smiling face, a cheerful mood, and polite language when they practice charity.

First of all, Christians ought to imagine themselves in the place of the person who needs their help, and they ought to sympathize with him as though they themselves were suffering; they ought to show real mercy and humaneness and offer their assistance as readily as if it were for themselves.

Heartfelt pity will banish arrogance and reproach, and will prevent contempt and domineering over the poor and the needy.

When a member of our physical body is diseased and the whole body has to labor to restore it to health, we do not despise this diseased member or hold it under obligation because it needs all this assistance.

3. The mutual help which the different parts of the body offer to each other is by the law of nature considered to be no favor, but a matter of course, which it would be cruel to refuse.

Therefore, if a man has performed one service, he should not reckon himself discharged of all other duties. A rich man, for instance, who has given away part of his property and leaves the burdens for others, cannot consider himself to be excused.

Every man, however important he may be, should realize that he is a debtor to his neighbor and that love demands that he give to the limit of his ability.

VIII. No happiness without God's blessing.

1. Let us discuss more in detail the main aspect of self-denial, its relation to God. It is needless to repeat the many remarks that have been made before, but it will suffice to point out how real self-denial makes us calm and patient.

First of all, Scripture draws our attention to this, that if we want ease and tranquility in our lives, we should resign ourselves and all that we have to the will of God, and at the same time we should surrender our affections to him as our Conqueror and Overlord.

To crave wealth and honor, to demand power, to pile up riches, to gather all those vanities which seem to make for pomp and empty display, that is our furious passion and our unbounded desire.

On the other hand, we fear and abhor poverty, obscurity, and humility, and we seek to avoid them by all possible means.

We can easily see how restless people are who follow their own mind, how many tricks they try and how they tire themselves out in their efforts to obtain the objects of their ambition and avarice, and then again to avoid poverty and humility.

2. If godfearing people do not want to be caught in such snares, they must pursue another course: they should not hope or desire or even think of prosperity without God's blessing.

We may believe and trust that everything depends on divine blessing alone.

It may look to us that we can easily attain honor and riches through our own industry or strenuous exertion or through the favor of others; yet, it is certain that all these things are nothing in themselves, and that we shall not make any headway by our insight or by our labors, but insofar as the Lord shall prosper both.

3. On the other hand, his blessing will find a way to make us happy and prosperous, whatever adversities may come.

And though we may be able to obtain a certain measure

no gain outside the gospel

of wealth and fame without divine blessing, as we may daily observe in godless people who acquire great honors and enormous riches, yet we shall see that those who are under the curse of God have not the smallest particle of happiness.

Therefore, we cannot gain anything without divine blessing; and if we do, it will prove a calamity to us.

Let us then not be foolish and wish for things that will make us more miserable.

IX. We should not be anxious to obtain riches and honors.

1. If we then believe that the whole cause of desirable prosperity is found in the divine blessing alone and that without this we may expect only miseries and calamities, it must be plain also that we should not anxiously strive for riches and honors by relying on our own diligence or cleverness or by depending on the favor of men or by trusting in the notion of good luck, but that we should always expect the Lord to direct us to the lot he has provided for us.

The result of this will be that, first of all, we shall not be in a rush to seize riches and honors by forbidden actions, by deceitful and criminal tricks, by robbing and injuring our neighbors; but that we shall limit ourselves to the pursuit of these interests which will not lure us away from the path of innocence.

For who can expect the help of divine blessing in fraud, robbery, and other evil acts?

2. As divine blessing comes only on him who is pure in his thoughts and righteous in his deeds, so it influences everyone who seeks to steer away from irregularity and corruption.

Further, we shall feel restrained from the intense desire to grow rich and from the false ambition to seek honors.

For would it not be shameful to trust in divine assistance, if at the same time we should crave matters that are against God's Word?

Far be it from God to prosper with his blessing what he curses with his mouth.

3. Finally, if we do not succeed according to our wishes and hopes, we shall, however, be kept from impatience and from detesting our condition, whatever it may be; because we shall understand that this would be rebellion against God at whose pleasure riches and poverty, honor and contempt are distributed.

In conclusion, he who retains God's blessing in the way we have described will not passionately pursue the things which man in general covets, and he will not use base methods from which he expects no advantage.

Moreover, a true Christian will not ascribe any prosperity to his own diligence, industry, or good fortune, but he will acknowledge that God is the author of it.

If he makes but small progress, or even suffers setbacks

while others are making headway, he will nevertheless bear his poverty with more calmness and moderation than any worldly man would feel when his success is average and contrary to his expectations.

4. A true Christian possesses a consolation which affords him more sweet satisfaction than the greatest wealth or power, because he believes that his affairs are so regulated by the Lord as to promote his salvation.

This was in the mind of David, who followed God and surrendered himself to his rule, and who declared, "I am as a child weaned of his mother; neither do I exercise myself in great matters, or in things too high for me" (Ps. 131:1–2).

X. The Lord is just in all his ways.

1. This is not the only case in which godfearing people should be quiet and patient, for they ought to try to live that way in all circumstances of life.

No one has rightly denied himself unless he has wholly resigned himself to the Lord and is willing to leave every detail to his good pleasure. If we put ourselves in such a frame of mind, then, whatever may happen to us, we shall never feel miserable or accuse God falsely because of our lot.

2. How necessary it is to train ourselves this way will become clear if we consider the numerous accidents to which we are exposed.

Diseases of all kinds come upon us, the one after the other: now the pestilence engulfs us, now the disasters of war are harassing us.

At another time frost or hail devours our crops, and we are threatened by scarcity and poverty.

Sometimes our dearest ones—husband, wife, parents, children, and other relatives—are snatched away by death, or our home is consumed by fire.

On account of such events people will curse their life and the day of their birth; they will blame the sun and the stars, and even reproach and blaspheme God as if he were cruel and unjust.

3. But a faithful believer will in all circumstances meditate on the mercy and fatherly goodness of God.

If he sees his relatives taken away from him and his home made lonesome, he must not cease to bless the Lord, and he had rather consider that the grace of God, which dwells in his home, will not leave it desolate.

Or, if he sees his grain fields and vineyards destroyed by frost or hail, and famine threatening him, he will not become discouraged and dissatisfied, but he will persist in this firm confidence: we are under the guardian care of our God, we are "the sheep of his pasture," and, therefore, he will supply us with the food we need.

If he shall be afflicted with illness, he will not be broken down with bitterness and give way to impatience and complain against God, but he will consider the justice and goodness of his Eternal Father and grow in patience while he is being chastened and corrected.

4. In short, knowing that whatever may happen is ordained by the Lord, he will receive it with a peaceful and thankful heart, that he may not be guilty of proudly resisting the rule of him to whom he has once committed himself and all his belongings.

Far be it from the heart of a Christian to accept the foolish and wretched consolation of the heathen philosophers who tried to harden themselves against adversity by blaming Fortune or Fate for it.

They thought that it was foolish to be displeased with our lot, because there is a blind and cruel power in the world which deals blows to everyone, worthy and unworthy.

But the principle of true devotion is that God alone is the Guide and Ruler of all prosperity and adversity, and that he is never in undue haste, but distributes all good and evil with the most equal justice (Ps. 79:13).

CHAPTER III

Patience
in
Crossbearing

I. Crossbearing is more difficult than self-denial.

1. Moreover, it is fitting for the faithful Christian to rise to a still higher level where Christ calls every disciple to "take up his cross."

For all whom the Lord has chosen and received into the society of his saints ought to prepare themselves for a life that is hard, difficult, laborious, and full of countless griefs.

It is the will of their heavenly Father to try them in this manner that he may test them.

He began with Christ, his firstborn Son, and he pursues this manner with all his children.

For though Christ was his most beloved Son, in whom the Father was always well pleased, yet we see that he was not treated with indulgence and tenderness, so that it may be truly said that he was not only continuously afflicted, but that his whole life was a perpetual cross.

2. The apostle explains the reason, that it was necessary for him to "learn obedience by the things which he suffered." Why then should we free ourselves from that condition to which Christ, our Chief, had to submit, especially since his submission was on our behalf, to give us an example of patience?

For the apostle teaches that it is the destiny of all God's children to "be conformed to him."

And it is a real comfort to us when we endure many miseries, which are called adversities and calamities, that we partake of the sufferings of Christ, in order that we may pass through our different tribulations as he escaped from an abyss of all evils to the glory of heaven.

3. For Saint Paul tells us that if we "know the fellowship of his sufferings" we shall also understand the "power of his resurrection"; and that, while we are "participating in his

death," we are also being prepared for sharing his glorious resurrection.

How much this helps to lighten the bitterness of the cross!

For the more we are afflicted by adversities, the more surely our fellowship with Christ is confirmed!

By this fellowship the adversities themselves not only become blessings to us, but they are also aids to greatly promote our happiness and salvation (Matt. 16:24; Matt. 3:17; 17:5; Heb. 5:8; Rom. 8:29; Acts 14:22; Phil. 3:10).

Continual cross

II. The cross makes us humble.

1. Our Lord was not compelled to bear the cross except to show and prove his obedience to his Father. But there are many reasons why we should live under a continual cross.

First, whereas we are naturally prone to attribute everything to our human flesh unless we have, as it were, object lessons of our stupidity, we easily form an exaggerated notion of our strength, and we take for granted that, whatever hardships may happen, we will remain invincible.

And so we become puffed up with a foolish, vain, and carnal confidence which arouses us to become haughty and proud toward God, as if our own power would be sufficient without his grace.

This vanity he cannot better repress than by proving to us from experience not only our folly, but also our extreme frailty.

Therefore he afflicts us with humiliation, or poverty, or loss of relatives, or disease, or other calamities.

Then, because we are unable to bear them, we soon are buried under them.

And so, being humbled, we learn to call upon his strength which alone makes us stand up under such a load of afflictions.

2. Even the greatest saints, though realizing that they can only be strong in the grace of God and not in themselves, are nevertheless more sure than they ought to be of their own bravery and persistence, unless he leads them by the trials of life into a deeper knowledge of themselves. This proud idea induced even David to say: "In my prosperity I said, I shall never be moved; Lord, by thy favor thou hast made my mountain to stand strong. Thou didst hide thy face, and I was troubled."

For he confesses that prosperity had so stupefied and benumbed his senses that he disregarded the grace of God on which he should have depended, relied on himself instead, and imagined that he could not fall.

3. If this happened to such a great prophet, who of us should not be fearful and cautious?

Though in prosperity many saints have flattered themselves with perseverance and patience, yet they learned that they had deceived themselves when adversity broke down their resistance.

Warned by such evidences of their spiritual illness, believers profit by their humiliations.

Robbed of their foolish confidence in the flesh, they take refuge in the grace of God.

And when they have done so, they experience the nearness of the divine protection which is to them a strong fortress (Ps. 30:6–7).

Hopeful

III. The cross makes us hopeful.

1. This is what Paul teaches, that "tribulation worketh patience, and patience, experience."

For God's promise to believers that he will help them in their trials, they experience to be true when they persist in their patience supported by his strength and not by their own.

Patience, therefore, affords a proof to the saints that God will actually give them the help he has promised whenever there is need.

And this also confirms their hope, for they certainly would be ungrateful if they did not rely for the future on the truth of God, which they have found to be sure and unchangeable.

Now we see what a stream of benefits flows from the cross. For if we discard the false opinions of our own virtue and discover our hypocrisy which leads us astray with its flatteries, our natural and pernicious pride tumbles down.

patience   51

When we are thus humbled, we are taught to rely on God alone, and we shall not stumble or sink down in despair.

From this victory we shall gather new hope, for when the Lord fulfills his promises, he confirms his truth for the future.

2. Though these were the only reasons, they are sufficient to show how necessary are the trials of the cross.

For it is no small profit to be robbed of our blind self-love so that we become fully aware of our weakness; to have such an understanding of our weakness that we distrust ourselves; to distrust ourselves to such an extent that we put all our trust in God; to depend with such boundless confidence on God that we rely entirely on his help, so that we may victoriously persevere to the end; to continue in his grace that we may know he is true and faithful in his promises; and to experience the certainty of his promises so that our hope may become firmer (Rom. 5:3–4).

IV. The cross teaches obedience.

1. The Lord has still another reason for afflicting his children: to try their patience and to teach them obedience.

Indeed, they cannot show any other obedience to him than the one he has given them; but he is pleased in this manner to exhibit and to test the graces which he has conferred on his saints, that they may not remain hidden and become useless.

When God's servants openly manifest his gifts of strength and firmness in their suffering, Scripture says that he is trying their patience.

Hence such expressions as "God tempted Abraham," who proved his devotion from the fact that he did not refuse to sacrifice his only son.

Therefore Peter states that our faith is tried by tribulations, just as gold is tried by fire in a furnace.

2. Who can deny that it is necessary that this most excellent gift of patience, which a believer has received from God, be developed by practice, so that he becomes sure and convinced of it?

For otherwise men would never esteem it as it deserves.

But if God himself acts justly when he prevents such virtues from becoming obscure and useless by offering us an occasion to exercise them, then this must be the best of reasons for trying the saints, for without affliction they would have no patience.

3. By the cross they are also instructed, I repeat, to obedience, because in this way they are taught to follow God's desire and not their own.

If everything proceeded according to their wishes, they would not understand what it means to follow God.

Seneca informs us that it was an ancient custom to exhort

people to bear adversity with patience by the maxim: "Follow God."

This implied that man submitted to the yoke of God only when he willingly accepted chastisement with the meekness of a child.

Therefore, if it is reasonable that we should show ourselves obedient in all things to our heavenly Father, then we certainly should not deny him the right to use every way to accustom us to practice this obedience (Gen. 22:1–2; 1 Pet. 1:7).

V. The cross makes for discipline.

1. Often we do not understand how necessary this obedience is for us, unless we also consider how eager our flesh is to shake off the yoke of the Lord as soon as we have been treated with some tenderness and indulgence.

For it is with us just as with unwilling horses, which first are pampered in idleness, and then grow fierce and untamable, and have no regard for the rider to whose reins they formerly submitted.

In other words, what the Lord complains of in his people Israel is continually seen in every one of us: When we are grown "fat" and "covered with fatness," we kick against him who has fed and cherished us.

The kindness of God ought to have led us to consider and love his goodness, but since we are so ungrateful that we are rather constantly spoiled by his indulgence, it is very necessary for us to be restrained by some discipline from breaking out into wilfulness.

2. Therefore, that we may not become haughty when we acquire wealth; that we may not become proud when we receive honors; that we may not become insolent when we are blessed with prosperity and health, the Lord himself, as he deems fit, uses the cross to oppose, restrain, and subdue the arrogance of our flesh.

And he does this by various means which are useful and wholesome for each of us.

For we are not all equally afflicted with the same disease or all in need of the same severe cure.

This is the reason why we see different persons disciplined with different crosses. The heavenly Physician takes care of the well-being of all his patients; he gives some a milder medicine and purifies others by more shocking treatments, but he omits no one; for the whole world, without exception, is ill (Deut. 32:15).

VI. The cross brings repentance.

1. Moreover, it is necessary that our most merciful Father should not only prevent our future weakness, but also correct our past offenses to keep us in the path of obedience.

Therefore, in every affliction, we ought immediately to review our past life.

When we do so we shall certainly find that we have deserved such chastisement.

Nevertheless, we should not draw the conclusion that we are first of all exhorted to patience because we should remember our sins.

For Scripture furnishes us a far better reason when it informs us that in adversity "we are chastened by the Lord, in order that we should not be condemned with the world."

2. Therefore, even in the bitterness of our trials we should acknowledge the mercy and kindness of our Father toward us; since even then he does not cease to promote our welfare.

For he does not afflict to destroy or ruin us, but rather to deliver us from the condemnation of the world.

This thought will lead us to what Scripture teaches in another place: "My son, despise not the chastening of the Lord, neither be weary of his correction; for whom the Lord loves he corrects, even as a father the son in whom he delights."

When we recognize the rod of a father, should we not show ourselves docile children rather than rebelliously imitate desperate men who have been hardened in their evil doings?

God would let us perish if he would not call us back to him by his corrections when we have failed, as the Apostle pointedly remarks, "If ye be without chastisement then are ye bastards, and not sons."

3. We are extremely perverse if we cannot bear with him when he shows his lovingkindness toward us and his great concern for our salvation.

Scripture points out this difference between believers and unbelievers; the latter, as old slaves of their incurable perversity, cannot endure the rod; but the former, like children of noble birth, profit by repentance and correction.

Now we must choose where we prefer to stand.

But having treated of this subject elsewhere let it suffice that I have touched on it here briefly (1 Cor. 11:32; Prov. 3:11–12; Heb. 12:8).

VII. Persecution brings God's favor.

1. It is a source of singular consolation for us when we suffer persecution "for righteousness' sake."

For then we ought to remember how greatly we are honored by God when he decorates us with the tokens of his service.

I call it persecution for righteousness' sake not only when we suffer in defense of the gospel, but also when we are opposed in upholding any just cause.

When we defend the truth of God over against the falsehoods of Satan, or protect good and innocent people against injustice and injury, it may be necessary for us to incur the hatred and indignation of the world, so that our lives, our possessions, or our reputations may be endangered.

But we should not be grieved when we exert ourselves in the service of God, and we should not count ourselves miserable when with his own mouth he calls us most blessed.

It is true that poverty by itself is misery; and the same may be said of exile, contempt, shame, and imprisonment; and finally, of all calamities death is the last and the worst.

But when God breathes his favor on us, all things work together for our happiness and our well-being.

Let us therefore be content with the approval of Christ rather than with the false opinion of our flesh.

Then we shall rejoice like the Apostles whenever he shall "count us worthy to suffer shame for his name."

2. What of it?

If we in our innocence and with a good conscience are robbed of our goods by the villainy of the wicked, and are reduced to poverty among men, we shall thereby increase our true riches with God in heaven.

If we are banished from our country, we shall be received into the intimate fellowship of God.

If we are tormented and despised, we shall be the more firmly rooted in Christ for fleeing to him.

If we are covered with reproach and shame, we shall receive the more glory in the Kingdom of God.

If we are massacred, we shall be received into the eternal glory.

God breathes his favor on us. [margin note]

We ought to be ashamed of deeming the everlasting values of less account than the shadowy and fleeing pleasures of the present life (Matt. 2:10; Acts 5:41).

VIII. Persecution should bring spiritual joy.

1. Since Scripture comforts us time and again in all maltreatments and misery which we may experience in the defense of a righteous cause, we may, therefore, be accused of extreme ingratitude if we do not receive these hardships from the hand of the Lord with resignation and spiritual joy; especially since this type of affliction, or cross, is most peculiar to believers.

For by our suffering Christ will be glorified in us according to the saying of Peter.

And since a haughty treatment to noble and independent minds is more intolerable than a hundred deaths, Paul warns us that not only persecution but also reproaches await us, just "because we trust in the living God."

And in another place he arouses us to follow his example and to go through "evil report and good report."

2. Moreover, we are not required to be cheerful while we shake off all sense of bitterness and sorrow.

The saints could not find any patience in cross bearing if they were not disturbed by sorrow and harassed with grief.

For instance, if there were no hardship in poverty, no agony in sickness, no distress in insults, no horror in death, what courage or moderation would it be to regard these afflictions with indifference?

But since each of them by its own bitterness bows down our hearts as a matter of course, the faithful will show their real strength by resisting and overcoming their grief, however much they may have to labor.

They will be patient when they are keenly provoked, and they will be restrained by the fear of God from any outbursts of intemperance.

Their joy and cheerfulness will be apparent when, wounded by sadness and sorrow, they will rest in the spiritual consolation of God (1 Pet. 4:14; 1 Tim. 4:10; 2 Cor. 6:8).

IX. The cross should not make us indifferent.

1. The struggle of believers against their natural emotions of sorrow while they try to build up patience and moderation has been fully described by Paul in these words: "We are troubled on every side, yet not distressed; we are perplexed, but not in despair; persecuted, but not forsaken; cast down, but not destroyed" (2 Cor. 4:8–9).

It is clear that bearing the cross patiently does not mean that we harden ourselves or do not feel any sorrow; according to the old notion of the Stoic philosophers that a great-hearted man is someone who has laid off his humanity, and who is not touched by adversity and prosperity, and not even by joy and sorrow, but who acts like a cold rock.

What profit is there in this proud wisdom?

They have pictured an image of patience which has never been found among men and which cannot exist, and in their desire to find a patience of a singular type they have removed it from human life.

2. At present there are among Christians modern Stoics who think it is wrong to groan and to weep and even to grieve in loneliness.

Such wild opinions generally come forth from men who are more dreamers than practical men, and who, therefore, cannot produce anything else but fantasies.

3. But we have nothing to do with such a harsh and rigorous philosophy which our Lord and Master Jesus has condemned in word and example.

For he mourned and wept for his own calamities as well as for those of others, and he did not teach his disciples any different way.

"The World," said he, "shall rejoice, but ye shall weep and lament."

And that no man might call sadness a vice, he has pronounced a blessing on them that mourn.

4. And no wonder, for if he condemned all tears, what must we judge of the Lord himself from whose body flowed tears of blood?

If every fear be labeled unbelief, what name shall we give to that anxiety of which we read that it depressed and amazed him?

If all sorrow is displeasing, how can we be pleased with his confession that his soul was "sorrowful even unto death" (John 16:20; Matt. 5:5; Luke 22:44)?

X. The cross makes for submission.

1. These things should be mentioned so that devout minds may be kept from despair; that they may not hurriedly give up their desires for patience because they cannot lay off their natural inclination toward sorrow. For despair will be the end of those who let their patience slip into indifference and who contend that a man is strong and courageous when he makes himself a senseless block. On the contrary, Scripture praises the saints for their patience when they are severely afflicted by their adversities, but not broken and overcome by them; when they are bitterly distressed, but nevertheless filled with spiritual joy; when they are weighed down by anxiety and become exhausted, and yet leap for joy because of the divine consolation.

Divine Consolation

2. At the same time there is a conflict in their hearts because our natural feelings avoid and fear what is hostile to our experience.

But our zeal for devotion struggles through our difficulties so that we become obedient to the divine will.

This conflict is expressed by the Lord when he addressed Peter as follows: "When you were young, you girded yourself, and walked where you would, but when you are old, another will gird you, and carry you where you would not."

It is not probable that Peter, when he was called to glorify God by his death, was led to it with reluctance and aversion; in this case his martyrdom would be entitled to little praise.

But, however much he might submit with the greatest eagerness of heart to the divine will, yet, because he had not shaken off his human feelings, he was distracted by an inner conflict.

For when he was thinking of the bloody death which was in store for him, he was stricken with fear and he would have gladly made his escape.

But, when he considered that God had called him to it, he suppressed this fear and submitted to it without reluctance and even with cheerfulness.

3. It must be our desire, therefore, if we want to be disciples of Christ, to fill our minds with such a great reverence for God and with such an unrestrained obedience that we may triumph over all contrary inclinations and submit to his plan.

In this way we shall remain constant in our patience, what-

Don't get whipped around by your feelings (handwritten)

Constant Submission (handwritten)

ever afflictions we may bear, and even in the greatest distress of our mind.

For adversity will always wound us with its stings.

When we are afflicted with disease we shall, therefore, groan and complain and pray for recovery.

When we are oppressed with poverty we shall feel lonely and sorry.

When we are defamed, despised, and offended, likewise we shall feel restless.

When we have to attend the funeral of our friends we shall shed tears.

4. But we must always come back to this consolation: The Lord planned our sorrow, so let us <u>submit to his will.</u>

Even in the throes of grief, groans, and tears, we must encourage ourselves with this reflection, so that our hearts may cheerfully bear up while the storms pass over our heads (John 21:18).

XI. The cross is necessary for our salvation.

1. Now that we have shown that the main consideration for bearing the cross is the divine will, we must finally point out briefly the difference between philosophical and Christian patience.

For very few of the philosophers have reached the high

understanding that we are subjected to afflictions by the divine hand, or have come to the conclusion that it is our duty to submit to his will.

And even those who have gotten so far do not mention any other reason than that resignation is a necessary evil.

What is this but stating that we must submit to God, because any effort to resist him is vain?

For if we obey God only from necessity, we will cease to obey as soon as we can escape from him.

2. But Scripture commands us to consider the divine will in a different light; first, as consistent with justice and fairness; then as directed to the perfection of our salvation.

The Christian exhortations to patience are, therefore, as follows: Whether we are afflicted with poverty, or exile, or imprisonment, or reproach, or disease, or loss of relatives, or any other similar calamity, we must remember that none of these things happen without the will and providence of God; and moreover, that he does nothing but with regular justice.

Do not our innumerable and daily sins deserve many more severe and grievous chastisements than those which he inflicts on us in his mercy?

Is it not very reasonable that our flesh should be subdued and that we should be accustomed to a yoke, so that our carnal impulses should not get the best of us and drive us into intemperance?

Are not the justice and truth of God worthy to be endured because of our sins?

We cannot without iniquity murmur or rebel.

We shall no longer hear that cold refrain of the philosopher that we must submit to necessity.

But we hear that lively and efficient appeal: We must obey because it is wrong to resist.

We must suffer patiently, because impatience is rebellion against the justice of God.

3. Because we really like nothing but what we imagine will profit and prosper us, our most merciful Father comforts us by this teaching that he promotes our salvation by inflicting the cross upon us.

If it be plain that adversities are good for us, why should we not then endure them with grateful and peaceful hearts?

For if we bear them patiently, we do not surrender to necessity, but we submit for our benefit.

The upshot of these considerations is that the more we are oppressed by the cross, the fuller will be our spiritual joy.

And, unavoidably, to this joy is attached thankfulness.

If praise and thanksgiving to the Lord can come forth only from a cheerful and joyful heart—and there is nothing which ought to repress such emotions—then it is evident that God will temper the bitterness of the cross by the joy of the Spirit.

Your cross

God refreshes/refines
us by the cross.
James 1:2

Chapter IV

Hopefulness
for the
Next World

I. There is no crown without a cross.

1. With whatever kind of trials we may be afflicted, we should always keep our eye on this goal, that we accustom ourselves to the contempt [of the vanities] of the present life in order that we may meditate on the future life.

For the Lord knows that we are by nature inclined to love this world blindly, and even carnally, and, therefore, he uses an excellent means to call us back and to arouse us from our sluggishness, that our hearts may not be too much attached to such a foolish inclination.

2. There is not one of us who does not strive passionately through the whole course of his life for the heavenly immortality, and who does not try to reach it.

For we are really ashamed that we are not better than the dumb animals, whose condition would not at all be inferior to ours if it were not for our hope in eternity after death.

But if we closely examine the ambitious plans, enterprises, and actions of every individual, we will find that they are all on the level of this earth.

Hence our stupidity that our mind, dazzled with the outward splendor of riches, power, and honor, cannot see beyond them.

The heart also, filled and distressed with avarice, ambition, and other evil desires, cannot rise above them.

In one word, the whole soul, wrapped up in carnal delights, seeks its happiness on this earth.

3. To counteract this, the Lord by various and severe lessons of misery, teaches his children the vanity of the present life.

That they may not promise themselves a life of ease and comfort, he permits them, therefore, to be frequently disturbed and molested by wars or revolutions, by robberies, and by other injuries.

That they may not hanker with too much avidity after passing and uncertain riches, or depend on what they possess, he reduces them to poverty, or at least limits them to mediocrity, sometimes by exile, sometimes by sterility of the land, sometimes by fire, sometimes by other means.

That they may not become too complacent or delighted in married life, he makes them distressed by the shortcomings of their partners, or humbles them through wilful offspring, or afflicts them with the want or loss of children.

But, if in all these matters he is more merciful to them, he shows them by diseases and dangers how unstable and passing all mortal blessings are, that they may not be puffed up with vain glory.

4. We, therefore, truly reap advantage from the discipline of the cross only when we learn that this life, taken by itself, is full of unrest, trouble, and misery, and not really happy from any point of view; and that all its so-called blessings are uncertain, passing, vain, and mixed with endless adversity.

In consequence of this we should at once come to the conclusion that nothing in this world can be sought or expected but strife, and that we must raise our eyes to heaven to see a crown.

But it must be admitted that our heart is never seriously inclined to wish for and to meditate on the future life unless it has first thoroughly learned to forsake the vanities of the present world.

II. We are inclined to overestimate the present life.

1. There is no golden mean between these two extremes; either this earthly life must become low in our estimation, or it will have our inordinate love.

Therefore, if we have any concern about eternity, we must put forth our most diligent efforts to free ourselves from our temporal chains.

Now, since the present life has numerous attractions, and much pleasure, beauty, and sweetness to delight us, it is most necessary for our highest interest that we should frequently be called away from it, that we may not be carried away by its glamour.

For what would be the outcome if we were constantly happy in the enjoyment of the blessings of this life?

We cannot even by the incessant round of evils be aroused to give enough thought to its miseries.

2. That human life is nothing but a vapor or shadow is not only known to the learned, but even the common people have many a proverb to that effect.

They consider this knowledge so useful that they have many striking phrases and rhymes about life and its vanity.

But there is scarcely anything which we more carelessly consider or sooner banish from our memory; for we go about everything as if we want to make ourselves immortal.

If we watch a funeral or walk among the graves, and thus

clearly see the image of death before our eyes, we philosophize, I confess, about the vanity of life.

And even that does not happen every day, for often we are not moved at all.

But when we are, our philosophy is only short-lived; it vanishes as soon as we go away and does not leave the smallest trace behind.

It passes out of existence like the applause for an entertaining program.

3. We not only forget death, but the fact that we are mortals, as if no word concerning this has ever reached us, and we continue our foolish dream that we are to live forever.

If any man in the meantime reminds us of the proverb that man is only a creature of a day, we are willing to acknowledge this truth, but with such lack of attention that the idea of perpetual life keeps on lingering in our minds.

4. Who, then, can deny that we need to be warned not only by words, but that we should be convinced by every possible evidence that the present life is full of miseries!

For even if after we have become convinced of this, we hardly know how to stop our perverse and foolish admiration of it, as if life were nothing but one great accumulation of blessings.

But if it is necessary for us to be taught by God, it certainly is also our duty to listen to him when he speaks and arouses us from our sluggishness, that we may turn our backs upon this world and try to meditate with all our heart on the life to come.

III. The blessings of this present life should not be despised.

1. Nevertheless, our constant efforts to lower our estimate of the present world should not lead us to hate life or to be ungrateful toward God.

For this life, though it is full of countless miseries, deserves to be reckoned among the divine blessings which should not be despised.

Therefore, if we discover nothing of God's goodness in it, we are already guilty of no small ingratitude toward him.

But to believers especially this life should be a witness of God's kindness, since all of it is destined to advance their salvation.

2. For, before he fully reveals to us the inheritance of eternal glory, he intends to show himself as our Father in matters of minor importance; and those are the blessings which he daily showers upon us.

Since this life, then, serves to teach us the divine kindness, should we dare to scorn it as if there were no particle of good in it?

We must, therefore, have enough sense and appreciation

to class it among the bounties of the divine love which should not be cast away.

For if Scriptural evidences were wanting, which are very numerous and clear, even nature itself urges us to give thanks to the Lord for having given us the light of life, and its many uses, and the means necessary to preserve it.

3. Moreover, we have far more reason to be thankful if we consider that this life helps to prepare us for the glory of the heavenly kingdom.

For the Lord has ordained that those who are to be crowned in heaven should first fight the good fight on earth, that they may not celebrate their triumph without actually having overcome the difficulties of warfare and having gained the victory.

Another reason is that here on earth we may have a foretaste of the divine kindness, so that our hope and longing may be kindled for the full revelation of it.

4. When we have come to this conclusion that our life in this world is a gift of God's mercy which we ought to remember with gratitude because we owe it to him, it will then be time for us to consider its misery.

For only in this way will we be delivered from an excessive joy of life to which we are by nature inclined, as we have observed before.

IV. What is earth, if compared with heaven?

1. Whatever glory we must subtract from the sinful love of life, we may add to the desire for a better world.

It is, indeed, true for pagans that the greatest blessing is not to be born, and the next, to die immediately.

For without knowledge of God and true religion, what else would they see in life but unhappiness and misery?

Nor was there anything unreasonable in the behavior of the Scythians, who mourned and wept at the birth of their relatives, and who solemnly celebrated at their funerals.

But their customs did not avail them in any respect, for without knowledge of true faith in Christ they did not understand how something which in itself is neither blessed nor desirable could be conducive to the benefit of the devout believers.

And so, the views of the pagans ended in despair.

2. It should be the purpose of believers, then, when they estimate this mortal life, that they understand that, as it is, it is nothing but misery.

For only then will they try diligently and with increasing cheerfulness and readiness to meditate on the future eternal life.

When we come to a comparison of heaven and earth, then we may indeed not only forget[1] all about the present life, but even despise and scorn it.

For, if heaven is our fatherland, what is this earth but a place of exile, and this life but a journey through a strange land?[2]

If leaving this world means the entrance into real life, what else is this world but a grave?

What else is dwelling on this sinful earth but being plunged into death?

If deliverance from the body means complete liberty, what is this body but a prison?

If to enjoy the presence of God is the peak of happiness, is it not misery to be without it?

For until we escape out of this world, "We are absent from the Lord."

Therefore, if the earthly life be compared to the heavenly, it should undoubtedly be despised and counted as a failure.

3. But the present life should never be hated, except insofar as it subjects us to sin, although even that hatred should not properly be applied to life itself.

However, we should become so wary and scornful of it that we may desire its end, though we should also be prepared to remain in it as long as it pleases the Lord.

In other words, our weariness should keep us from fretting and impatience.

For this life is a post at which the Lord has placed us, and we must stay at it until the Lord calls us away.

Paul, indeed, laments his lot that he is kept in the bondage of the body longer than he would wish, and he ardently sighs for deliverance.

At the same time he rests in the will of God, and states that he is ready for either, to stay or to leave.

He acknowledges that he is bound to glorify the name of God, either by life or by death, but that it belongs to the Lord to determine what is most expedient for his glory.

4. Therefore, if it is fitting for us "to live and to die for the Lord," let us leave the limits of our life and death to his decision and good pleasure.

At the same time let us ardently desire and continually meditate on death while we despise [the vanities of] the present life in comparison with future immortality.

And let us on account of our enslavement to sin wish to leave this life whenever it will please the Lord (2 Cor. 5:6; Rom. 7:24; Phil. 1:20; Rom. 14:7–8).

V. We should not fear death, but lift up our heads.

1. It is terrible that many who boast themselves to be Christians, instead of longing for death, are so filled with fear of it that they tremble whenever the word is mentioned, as if it were the greatest calamity that could befall them.

It should not surprise us, indeed, if our natural feeling should be alarmed at hearing of our separation from this life.

But it is intolerable that there should not be sufficient light and devotion in a Christian's breast to suppress all that fear with an overwhelming consolation.

For if we consider that this unstable, depraved, perishable, frail, withering, and corrupt tabernacle of our body is dissolved, in order that it may hereafter be restored to a durable, perfect, incorruptible, and heavenly glory—will not our faith then induce us to wish ardently for what nature dreads?

If we remember that by death we are called back from exile to home, to our heavenly fatherland, shall we then not be filled with comfort?

2. But it will be said, there is nothing in this world that does not want to be permanent.

It must be admitted, but for that very reason we should look forward to a future immortality, where we may obtain such a realm of stability as is not found on this earth.

For Paul clearly teaches believers to go with anxious longing toward death, not to be stripped of our body but to be clothed with a new garment.

Shall brute animals, and even lifeless creatures, down to blocks and stones, aware of their present vanity, be looking forward to the resurrection at the last day, that they may be delivered from vanity, together with the children of God; and shall we, gifted with the light of natural reason and with the far superior enlightenment of the Spirit of God; shall we, when we consider our future existence, not lift our minds above the corruption of this world?

3. But, it is not necessary or suitable for my present purpose to argue against such utter perverseness as fear of death.

In the beginning I have already declared that I would not enter on a complicated discussion of commonplace topics.

I would persuade such timid hearts to read Cyprian's treatise on *Mortality*, unless they should deserve to be referred to philosophers, that they may blush when they discover how even pagans despise death.

But this we may positively state, that nobody has made any progress in the school of Christ unless he cheerfully looks forward to the day of his death and to the day of the final resurrection.

4. For Paul stamps this mark on all believers, and Scripture often calls our attention to it when it wants to provide us with a motive for true joy.

"Look up," says the Lord, "and lift up your heads, for your redemption draws nigh."

Is it reasonable to expect that the things which he planned to arouse us to ecstasy and wide-awakeness should cause us nothing but sorrow and consternation?

If this is the case, why do we still glory in him as our Master?

Let us, therefore, return to a sounder judgment, and notwithstanding the opposition of the blind and stupid desires of our flesh, let us not hesitate to long passionately for the coming of our Lord, as the most stirring of all events.

And let us not only long for it, but even groan and sigh for [the day of judgment].[3]

For he shall come to us as a Savior, to deliver us from this bottomless maelstrom of all evils and miseries, and he shall guide us into the blessed inheritance of his life and glory (2 Cor. 5:4; Titus 2:13; Luke 21:28).

VI. The Lord will come in his glory: *Maranatha.*

1. It is true beyond doubt that the whole family of believers, as long as they are living on the earth, must be "accounted as sheep for the slaughter," in order that they may become more and more like Christ their Head.

Their condition, therefore, would be extremely deplorable if they would not raise their thoughts toward heaven, rise above the passing show, and look beyond the horizon of this world.

2. Let the impious flourish in their riches and honors, and enjoy their so-called peace of mind.

Let them boast of their splendor and luxury, and abound in every joy.

Let them harass the children of light with their wickedness, let them insult them with their pride, let them rob them by their greed, let them provoke them with their utter lawlessness.

But when the believers see this, let them lift their eyes

above this world, and they will not have any difficulty to maintain their peace of heart under such calamities.

For they will look forward to the day when the Lord will receive his faithful servants into his kingdom of peace.

Then he will wipe every tear from their eyes, clothe them with robes of joy, adorn them with crowns of victory, entertain them with infinite delights, exalt them to his glory, and make them partakers of his own happiness.

3. But the evildoers who have been great in this world he will hurl down into the abyss of shame.

He will change their delights into torments, and their laughter and mirth into weeping and gnashing of teeth.

He will disturb their rest with dreadful agonies of conscience.

He will plunge them with their adulteries into the unquenchable fire, and put them in subjection to the faithful whose patience they have abused.

For, according to Paul, it is a righteous thing with God to award punishment to them that trouble the saints, and to give rest to those who are troubled, when the Lord Jesus shall be revealed from heaven.

4. This is our only consolation.

If we are deprived of this we shall have to sink into despair, or comfort ourselves with the vain pleasures of this world.

For even the Psalmist confesses that he was confounded

when he kept on wondering about the present prosperity of the wicked.

And he could not regain his composure until he entered the sanctuary and marked the latter end of the righteous and the unrighteous.

To conclude in a few words:

The cross of Christ triumphs only in the hearts of believers over the devil and the flesh, over sin and wickedness, when they lift their eyes to behold the power of the resurrection (Rom. 8:36; 1 Cor. 15:19; Isa. 25:8; Rev. 7:17; 2 Thess. 1:6–7; Ps. 73:2ff).

CHAPTER V

The Right Use
of the
Present Life

I. Let us avoid extremes.

1. Just as Scripture points us to heaven as our goal, so it fully instructs us in the right use of earthly blessings, and this ought not to be overlooked in a discussion of the rules of life.

For if we must live, we must also use the necessary instruments for life.

We cannot even avoid those matters which serve our pleasures rather than our needs.

But that we may use them with a pure conscience, we should observe moderation, whether we mean the one or the other.

2. This the Lord prescribes in his Word, when he teaches us that for his servants the present life is like a pilgrimage in which they are traveling toward the heavenly kingdom.

Even if this earth is only a vestibule, we ought undoubtedly to make such a use of its blessings that we are assisted rather than delayed in our journey.

It is not without reason, therefore, that Paul advises us to use this world as if we did not use it, and to buy possessions in the same frame of mind as when we sell them.

3. But as this is a moot question, and as we run the danger of falling into two opposite errors, let us try to proceed on safe ground, so that we may avoid both extremes.

For there have been some people, otherwise good and holy, who saw that intemperance and luxury time and again drive man to throw off all restraints unless he is curbed by the utmost severity.

And in their desire to correct such a pernicious evil they have adopted the only method which they saw fit, namely to permit earthly blessings only insofar as they were an absolute necessity.

This advice showed the best of intentions but was far too rigid.

For they committed the very dangerous error of imposing on the conscience of others stricter rules than those laid down in the Word of the Lord.

By restricting people within the demands of necessity, they meant abstinence from everything possible.

According to them, it would be scarcely permissible to eat and drink anything but dry bread and pure water.

Others sought even greater rigidity, like Crates of Thebes, of whom it is told that he threw his treasures into the sea out of fear that unless they were destroyed he himself would be ruined by them.

4. On the other hand, there are many nowadays who seek a pretext to excuse intemperance in the use of external things, and who desire to indulge the lusts of the flesh.

Such people take for granted that liberty should not be restricted by any limitations at all; but to this we can never agree.

They clamor that it ought to be left to the conscience of every individual to use as much as he thinks fit for himself.

5. We must grant, indeed, that it is not right or possible to bind the consciences of others with hard and fast rules.

But, since Scripture lays down some general principles for the lawful use of earthly things, we certainly ought to follow them in our conduct (1 Cor. 7:30–31).

II. Earthly things are gifts of God.

1. The first principle we should consider is that the use of gifts of God cannot be wrong, if they are directed to the same purpose for which the Creator himself has created and destined them.

For he has made the earthly blessings for our benefit, and not for our harm.

No one, therefore, will observe a more proper rule than he who will faithfully observe this purpose.

2. If we study, for instance, why he has created the various kinds of food, we shall find that it was his intention not only to provide for our needs, but likewise for our pleasure and for our delight.

In clothing he did not only keep in mind our needs, but also propriety and decency.

In herbs, trees, and fruit, besides being useful in various ways, he planned to please us by their gracious lines and pleasant odors.

For if this were not true, the psalmist would not enumerate among the divine blessings "the wine that makes glad the heart of man, and the oil that makes his face to shine."

And the Scriptures would not declare everywhere that he has given all these things to mankind that they might praise his goodness.

3. Even the natural properties of things sufficiently point out to what purpose and to what extent we are allowed to use them.

Should the Lord have attracted our eyes to the beauty of the flowers and our sense of smell to pleasant odors, and should it then be sin to drink them in?

Has he not even made the colors so that the one is more wonderful than the other?

Has he not granted to gold and silver, to ivory and marble a beauty which makes them more precious than other metals or stones?

In one word, has he not made many things worthy of our attention that go far beyond our needs (Ps. 104:15)?

III. True gratitude will restrain us from abuse.

1. Let us discard, therefore, that inhuman philosophy which would allow us no use of creation unless it is absolutely necessary.

Such a malignant notion deprives us of the lawful enjoyment of God's kindness. And, it is impossible actually to accept it, until we are robbed of all our senses and reduced to a senseless block.

On the other hand, we must with equal zeal fight the lusts of the flesh, for if they are not firmly restrained, they will transgress every bound.

As we have observed, licentiousness has its advocates: there are people who under the pretext of liberty will stop short of nothing.

2. First of all, if we want to curb our passions we must remember that all things are made for us, with the purpose that we may know and acknowledge their Author.

We should praise his kindness toward us in earthly matters by giving him thanks.

But what will become of our thanksgiving if we indulge in dainties or wine in such a way that we are too dull to carry out the duties of devotion or of our business?

Where is our acknowledgment of God, if the excesses of our body drive us to the vilest passions and infect our mind with impurity, so that we can no longer distinguish between right and wrong?

Where is our gratitude toward God for clothing if we admire ourselves and despise others because of our own sumptuous apparel?

Where is it if we prepare ourselves for unchastity with the elegance and beauty of our dress?

Where is our acknowledgment of God if our thoughts are fixed on the glamour of our garments?

3. For many so madly pursue pleasure that their minds become enslaved to it.

Many are so delighted with marble, gold, and painting, that they become like statues.

They are, as it were, transfixed into metal, and begin to resemble colorful idols.

The flavor of meats and the sweetness of odors make some people so stupid that they have no longer any appetite for spiritual things.

And this holds for the abuse of all other natural matters.

Therefore, it is clear, that the principle of gratitude should curb our desire to abuse the divine blessings.

This principle confirms the rule of Paul, that we may "not make provision for the flesh to fulfill its lusts,"

For if we give our natural desires free rein, they will pass all the bounds of temperance and moderation (Rom. 13:14).

IV. Let us live with moderation.

1. But there is no surer and shorter way [to gratitude] than to turn our eyes away from the present life and to meditate on the immortality of heaven.

From this flow two general principles:

The first is "that they that have wives be as though they had none; and they that buy as though they possessed not; and they that use this world as not abusing it," according to the precept of Paul.

The second is that we should learn to bear poverty quietly and patiently, and to enjoy abundance with moderation.

2. He who commands us to use this world as though we used it not, forbids not only all intemperance in eating and drinking, and excessive pleasure, ambition, pride, and fastidiousness in our furniture, home, and apparel, but every care and affection which would drag down our spiritual level or destroy our devotion.

It was in olden times truly observed by Cato, that there is great concern about the appearance of the body but great carelessness about virtue.

There is also an old proverb, that they who pay much attention to the body generally neglect the soul.

3. Therefore, though the liberty of believers in external things cannot be restricted by hard and fast rules, yet it is surely subject to this law, that they should indulge as little as possible.

On the contrary, we should continually and resolutely exert ourselves to shun all that is superfluous and avoid all vain display of luxury.

We should zealously beware that anything the Lord gave us to enrich life become a stumbling block (1 Cor. 7:29–31).

V. Let us be patient and content under privation.

1. The other principle will be that people who are poor should learn to be patient under privations, that they may not be tormented by a passion for riches.

Those who regard this moderation have made no small progress in the school of the Lord, and those who have not made this progress have scarcely given any proof of their discipleship in Christ.

2. For not only is a passion for earthly things accompanied by almost all other vices, but he who is impatient under privation will commonly betray the opposite vice when he is in luxury.

This means that he who is ashamed of a simple garment will be proud of a glamorous one.

He who is not content with a sober meal feels uneasy because he desires a sumptuous one, and will even be intemperate as soon as there is an occasion.

He who grows restless and dissatisfied while he puts up with privation and humility will not be able to guard against pride and arrogance if he rides to honor.

Therefore, let all those who want to be sincere in their devotion, earnestly try to follow the apostolic example, "both to be full and to be hungry, both to abound and to suffer need" (Phil. 4:12).

3. Scripture also mentions a third principle by which the use of earthly things is limited, and this was mentioned when we spoke of the precepts of self-denial.

For while all such things are given to us by divine kindness and are meant to be for our benefit, they are at the same time like deposits entrusted to our care, and of these we shall have to give an account someday.

We ought to manage them, therefore, in such a way as if we incessantly heard this warning in our ears: "give an account of your stewardship."

4. Let us also remember who demands this account.

It is he who so highly recommends restraint, sobriety, frugality, and modesty.

It is he who abhors excess, pride, showiness, and vain display.

It is he who will not approve our management of his blessings unless we are urged on by love.

It is he who with his own mouth condemns all pleasures which lead us away from chastity and purity, and which make us foolish and stupid (Phil. 4:12; Luke 6:2).

VI. Be faithful in your divine calling.

1. Finally we should note that the Lord commands every one of us in all the actions of our life to be faithful in our calling.

For he knows that the human mind burns with restlessness, that it is swept easily hither and thither, and that its ambition to embrace many things at once is insatiable.

Therefore, to prevent that general confusion being produced by our folly and boldness, he has appointed to every-one his particular duties in the different spheres of life.

And, that no one might rashly go beyond his limits, he has called such spheres of life vocations, or callings.

Every individual's sphere of life, therefore, is a post assigned him by the Lord that he may not wander about in uncertainty all the days of his life.

And so necessary is this distinction, that in his sight all our actions are measured by it, and often very differently from the judgment of human reason or philosophy.

2. There is no greater heroism even among philosophers than to deliver one's country from tyranny.

But the voice of the heavenly Judge openly condemns the private man who kills a tyrant.

It is not within our plan to enumerate examples, but let it be sufficient to know that the principle and basis of right conduct in every civil case is our calling by the Lord.

He who disregards his calling will never keep the straight path in the duties of his work.

Sometimes he may perhaps succeed in doing something that appears to be praiseworthy.

But however good it may look in the eyes of man, before the throne of God it will not be acceptable.

And besides, there will be no consistency in the various parts of his life.

3. Our present life, therefore, will be best regulated if we always keep our calling in mind.

No one will then be tempted by his own boldness to dare to undertake what is not compatible with his calling, because he will know that it is wrong to go beyond his limits.

Anyone who is not in the front ranks should be content to accomplish his private task, and should not desert the place where the Lord has put him.

It will be no small comfort for his cares, labors, troubles, and other burdens, when a man knows that in all these matters God is his guide.

The magistrate will then carry out his office with greater willingness.

The father of a family will then perform his duties with more courage.

And everyone in his respective sphere of life will show more patience, and will overcome the difficulties, cares, miseries, and anxieties in his path, when he will be convinced that every individual has his task laid upon his shoulders by God.

If we follow our divine calling, we shall receive this unique consolation that there is no work so mean and so sordid that does not look truly respectable and highly important in the sight of God (*Coram Deo!*) (Gen. 1:28; Col. 1:1ff)!

Notes

Chapter I: *Humble Obedience, the True Imitation of Christ*

1. Calvin inserts here: "I am not fit to write copiously, because I love brevity. But I might try in the future; and, otherwise, I shall leave the task to others."

2. Calvin evidently thinks here of 1 Corinthians 1, 2, and 3.

Chapter IV: *Hopefulness for the Next World*

1. The French has *pass by lightly*; the Latin has *neglect.*
2. The Latin has the first; the French the second main clause.
3. Added in French.

? Love the sinner
  hate the sin